Plants and Living Together

by Jocelyn Vial

PEARSON
Scott
Foresman

DK

How do living things interact?

Ways Living Things Interact

Living things interact in many ways. An interaction between them can be helpful. It may help a living thing survive. Animals living in groups help each other. One kind of living thing may help another. Two different kinds of living things may help each other.

Honey bees interact in their hive.

Think about these examples. Many animals live together in herds. The animals of the herd protect each other. Flowers need light to grow. Sometimes flowers grow on trees. Then they can get more light. Insects drink nectar from flowers. When they do this, they spread the flowers' pollen to other flowers.

Members of a herd protect each other.

A tree helps a flower get light.

An insect gets nectar. It spreads the plant's pollen.

Living in Groups

Some plants and animals live in groups. Members of the group protect each other from predators.

For example, prairie dogs live in groups. A prairie dog whistles if it senses danger, such as a predator. This tells the whole group of prairie dogs to run and hide. They stay hidden until the danger is gone.

These fish live in a group. How do you think the fish help each other?

One Living Thing Helping Another

Sometimes an interaction helps only one thing. A barnacle is a small animal. It attaches to the skin of a whale. As the whale swims, the barnacle opens its shell to catch food. The whale helps the barnacle get food. But the barnacle does not help the whale in any way.

Helping One Another

In some interactions, different kinds of living things are partners. They help each other.

The yucca moth helps the yucca plant. The moth moves pollen from one yucca to another.

The plant also helps the moth. It gives the moth a place to lay its eggs. It also gives the moth food for its young.

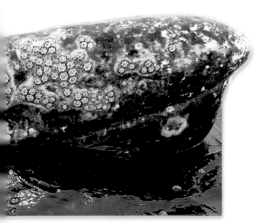

Barnacle

Yucca moth and yucca plant

How do living things get energy?

Sources of Energy

A living thing that makes its own food is a **producer.** All green plants are producers. They make food by using energy from sunlight. They also use matter from air and soil.

Some living things cannot make their own food. They get energy from the food they eat. A living thing that eats food is a **consumer.**

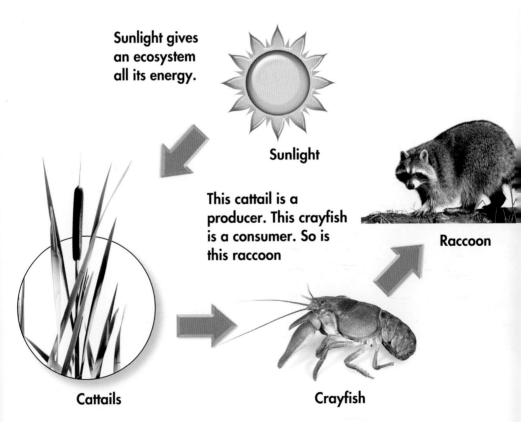

Sunlight gives an ecosystem all its energy.

Sunlight

This cattail is a producer. This crayfish is a consumer. So is this raccoon

Raccoon

Cattails

Crayfish

Do you know which of these animals is an omnivore? The bear! A wolf eats only meat. It's a carnivore. Sheep are herbivores. They eat only plants.

Kinds of Consumers

A consumer that eats only plants is an **herbivore.** A consumer that eats only animals is a **carnivore.** Some consumers eat both plants and animals. This type of consumer is an **omnivore.**

Food Chains

The cattail, crayfish, and raccoon make up a food chain. A food chain is a group of producers and consumers that interact. The crayfish eats the cattail. It gets food energy from the plant. Then the crayfish becomes prey for the raccoon. **Prey** is any animal that others hunt for food. An animal that hunts food is a **predator.** Energy moves from producers to prey to predators. Each organism gives off some of this energy as heat.

A cattail uses energy from the Sun to make food.

The crayfish eats the cattails.

The raccoon eats the crayfish.

Energy in a Food Web

Two or more food chains make a food web. Energy moves in many different ways in a food web. A Great Plains food web is pictured below.

A Changing Food Web

When one part of a food web changes, other parts change. What would happen if prairie dogs were removed from the web? Ferrets would not have enough food. They would start to die out. Animals that eat ferrets would have to find other food. This could affect the mouse population.

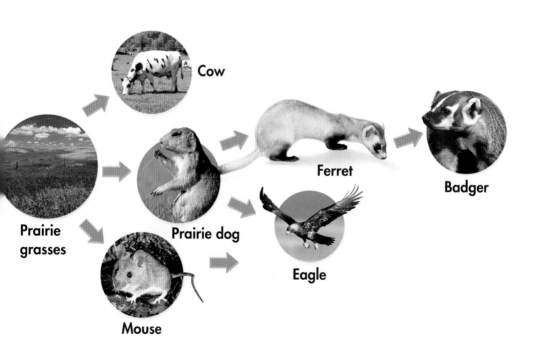

Cow

Ferret

Badger

Prairie grasses

Prairie dog

Eagle

Mouse

How do living things compete?

Competing for Resources

When two or more living things need the same resource, they are in **competition.** Living things compete for food, water, sunlight, and living space.

Predators and Prey

Groups of predators compete for prey. Hunting birds are one example. Faster, stronger birds may catch more prey or steal prey from other birds.

Prey also compete. A strong deer has a better chance of escaping a predator.

What are these animals competing for?

Other Kinds of Competition

Living things compete for space. Purple loosestrife is a plant that takes space from other plants in many places. Some animals compete with humans for space.

Living things also compete for oxygen. Sometimes too many algae grow in a pond, lowering oxygen levels. Animals must compete for the oxygen left.

Competition can follow a cycle. If there is not enough food, the population of animals will decrease. When there are fewer animals needing food, the number of plants can increase. The cycle begins again.

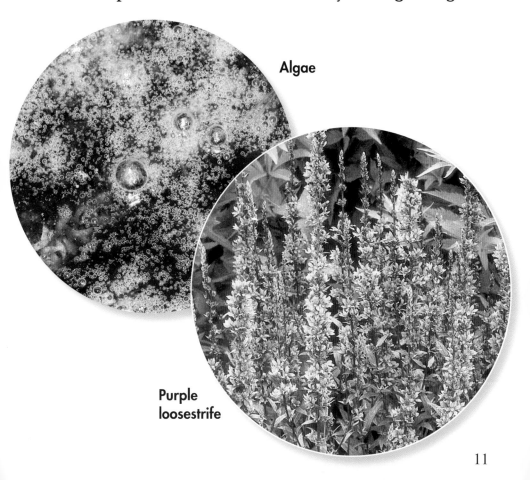

Algae

Purple
loosestrife

How do environments change?

Causes of Change

Living things can change their environment. A beaver builds a dam across a stream. The dam floods many dry places. It forms a wetland. Fish and birds can live in the wetland. But animals who lived on the dry land must move. Those animals must find new homes. Some may not survive.

How is this beaver changing the environment?

Natural events such as droughts, hurricanes, and floods, can also change environments. Little rain falls during a drought. Plants and animals may not get enough water during droughts. Hurricanes can wash away beaches, knock trees over, and cause flooding. A flood can kill plants, spread mud, move good soils, and destroy animals' homes.

How have these environments changed?

Drought

Hurricane

Flood

Living Things Return

In 1980 the volcano Mt. St. Helens erupted in the state of Washington. The blast knocked down and burned trees. It sent mud and rocks sliding. Few living things survived in the area of the eruption.

Over time, wind carried seeds to Mt. St. Helens. New plants grew. Animals returned. Today Mt. St. Helens is filled with life. But the mountain could erupt again.

Forest fires can destroy habitats in the same way. Forest fires may also improve habitats for existing plants and animals.

Mt. St. Helens changed the environment. But living things returned.

Patterns of Change

Living things change together. Often the changes happen in patterns. For example, trees grow old, die, and fall. Decomposers feed on the dead trees. A **decomposer** is a living thing that breaks down living things that have died. This is called **decay.** Decay can make the soil good for growing new trees. These trees will die someday and decay also. The life cycles of the two different trees are connected.

Decay makes it possible for new trees to grow.

These mushrooms cause decay.

What is a healthy environment for people?

What People Need

People need many things to live. They get these things from the environment.

People need food. Most people buy their food. It comes from farms and ranches.

People need shelter. Shelter protects people from the weather.

People need clean water. Many people get their water from special lakes. These lakes are called reservoirs.

Do you know where your food and water come from?

People need air. The air is often cleaner outside cities.

People need a clean environment. To keep it clean, waste must be removed. Garbage and other waste go to different places. Some towns and cities put garbage in a landfill.

Healthful Foods

Eating healthful foods helps people get all the vitamins, minerals, and other nutrients their bodies need.

Look at the picture below. It shows some of the foods that your body needs, such as fruit, vegetables, dairy food, and fish. You should also eat whole grains, nuts, eggs, and meat. Food should be fresh, clean, and stored properly.

Is this the kind of food you eat?

From Food to Energy

When you eat food, your digestive system goes to work. It breaks food down. It turns food into a form your body can use.

Look at the drawing. It shows the main parts of the digestive system. They turn food you eat into energy you need to live and grow!

Food is crushed in your mouth and then mixed with digestive juices in your stomach. Your small intestine does most digesting. It also moves particles into your blood. The large intestine removes food you cannot use.

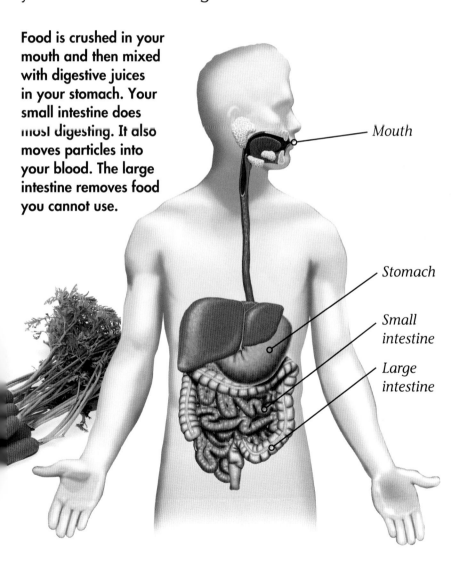

Mouth

Stomach

Small intestine

Large intestine

How can people stay healthy?

Exercise

Exercise, like healthful foods, builds healthy bodies. People get exercise in different ways. They may swim or skate. They may clean the house or rake the yard.

Exercise helps keep your heart, lungs, and muscles strong. These are important parts of your body's systems.

Exercise keeps people in shape. People who are in shape have more energy. They can work and play. They can feel good about themselves.

It's important to try to stay healthy. You can stay healthy by eating good foods. You can also stay healthy by getting enough exercise and rest.

What is your favorite kind of exercise?

Avoiding Germs

Have you ever had the flu? The flu is an illness caused by germs.

Germs are very small living things or particles. Viruses and bacteria are germs. Many germs can cause disease. A **disease** is when your body or part of your body does not work properly.

Most illnesses are not dangerous. Still, it's better to be healthy than to be sick!

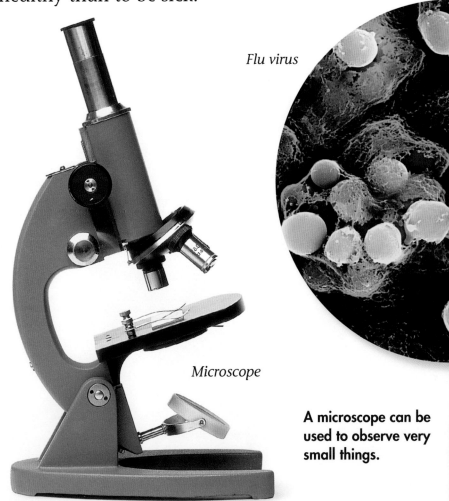

Flu virus

Microscope

A microscope can be used to observe very small things.

Stopping the Spread of Germs

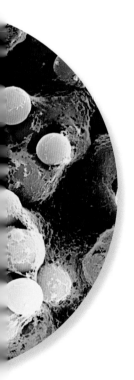

You can do many things to stop the spread of germs. Just follow these simple rules. First, stay home from school when you are ill. Second, wash your hands often. Third, cover your nose and mouth when you sneeze or cough. Fourth, clean and cover all cuts and scrapes.

Glossary

carnivore a consumer that eats only animals

competition when two or more living things need the same resource

consumer a living thing that eats food

decay the breakdown of waste and things that have died

decomposer a living thing that breaks down waste and things that have died

disease when your body or a part of your body does not work properly

germs very small living things that can make people ill

herbivore a consumer that eats only plants

omnivore a consumer that eats both plants and animals

predator a consumer that hunts for food

prey any animal that is hunted by others for food

producer a living thing that makes its own food